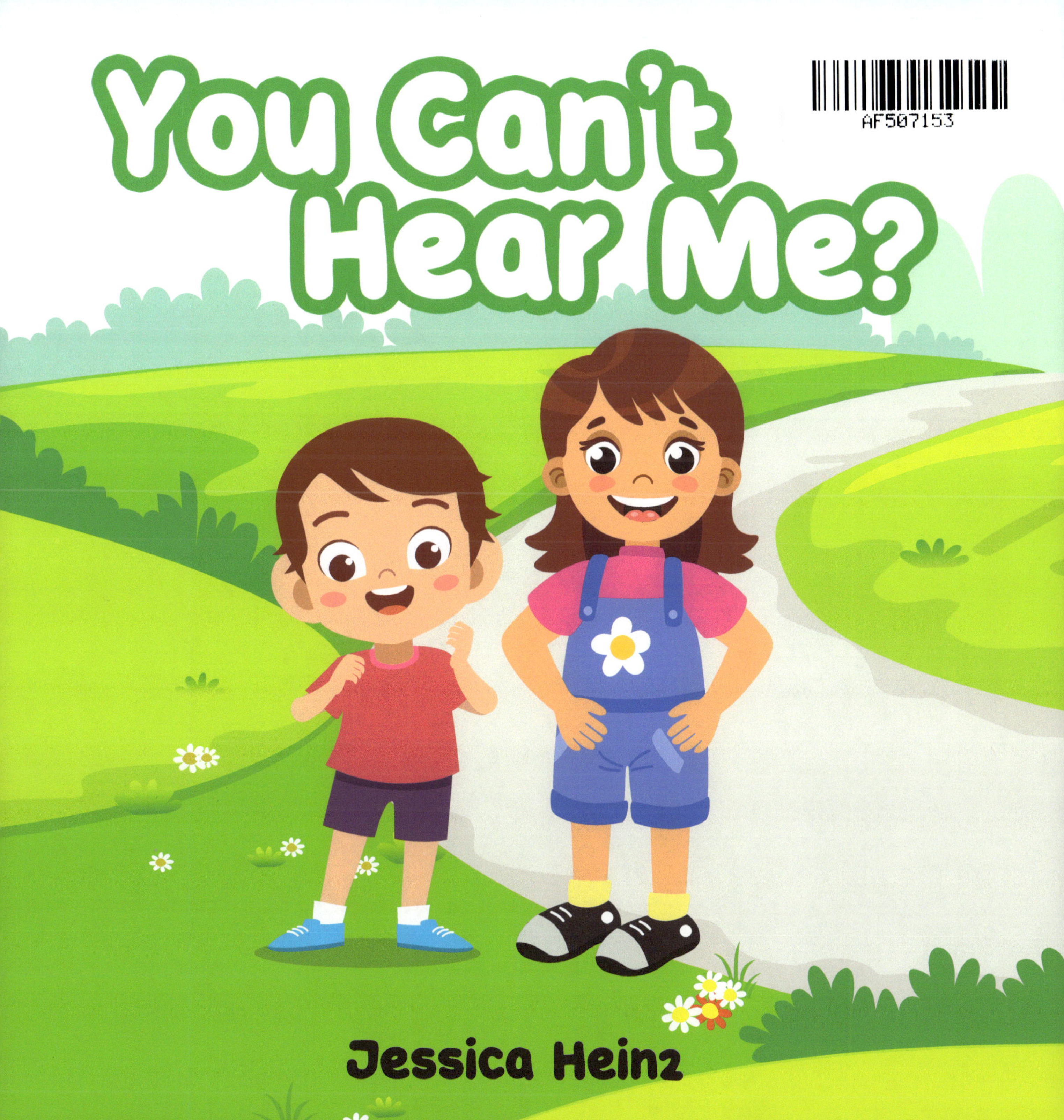

# You Can't Hear Me?

## Jessica Heinz

# Dedication

To my entire family, who have inspired me to connect
with others in my own way.

# Acknowledgements

Mom, Dad, and my husband – for supporting my adventures, taking chances, and keeping me grounded.

# About the Author

Jessica Heinz is a genetic counseling student with a keen interest in promoting inclusivity and understanding within the deaf community. Inspired by her academic research and personal advocacy, Jessica explores the intersection of medical advancements and cultural preservation. She is particularly passionate about raising awareness of the challenges and richness of deaf culture in an ever-evolving society.

Jessica's debut children's book, You Can't Hear Me?, introduces young readers to the power of communication and the importance of empathy, regardless of language or ability. Through her work, she hopes to inspire a deeper appreciation for diversity and foster meaningful connections among individuals of all abilities.

When not studying or writing, Jessica enjoys engaging with community outreach programs and finding creative ways to bridge the gap between science and culture.

Mia was excited to meet new friends at the playground. There were so many kids to play with!

Mia saw a new kid playing by themselves in the sandbox.
She walked over with a big smile.

"Hi, I'm Mia!" she said loudly,
but Alex didn't seem to hear her.

Mia tried again, but Alex didn't respond.
Mia felt confused.

Another kid came over. "Alex is deaf.
That means they can't hear you like we do."

"Oh!" said Mia.
"How can I talk to Alex then?"

"We can use our hands to talk," the friend said.
"I'll show you!"

Mia practiced the signs with her friend.
"This is fun!" she said, giggling.

Mia went back to Alex. She waved and signed,
"Hello!" Alex's face lit up.

"Do you want to play?" Mia signed, smiling.
Alex nodded excitedly.

They took turns making funny faces and
showing each other signs.

Mia learned that even without words,
she could talk to her new friend.

Mia noticed some other kids watching her and Alex.
She waved them over. "Do you want to learn to sign too?"

Mia taught them a few signs like "Hello," "Friend," and "Play." Everyone practiced together, laughing and learning.

Soon, everyone was signing and playing together.
Mia knew she had made new friends in a special way!

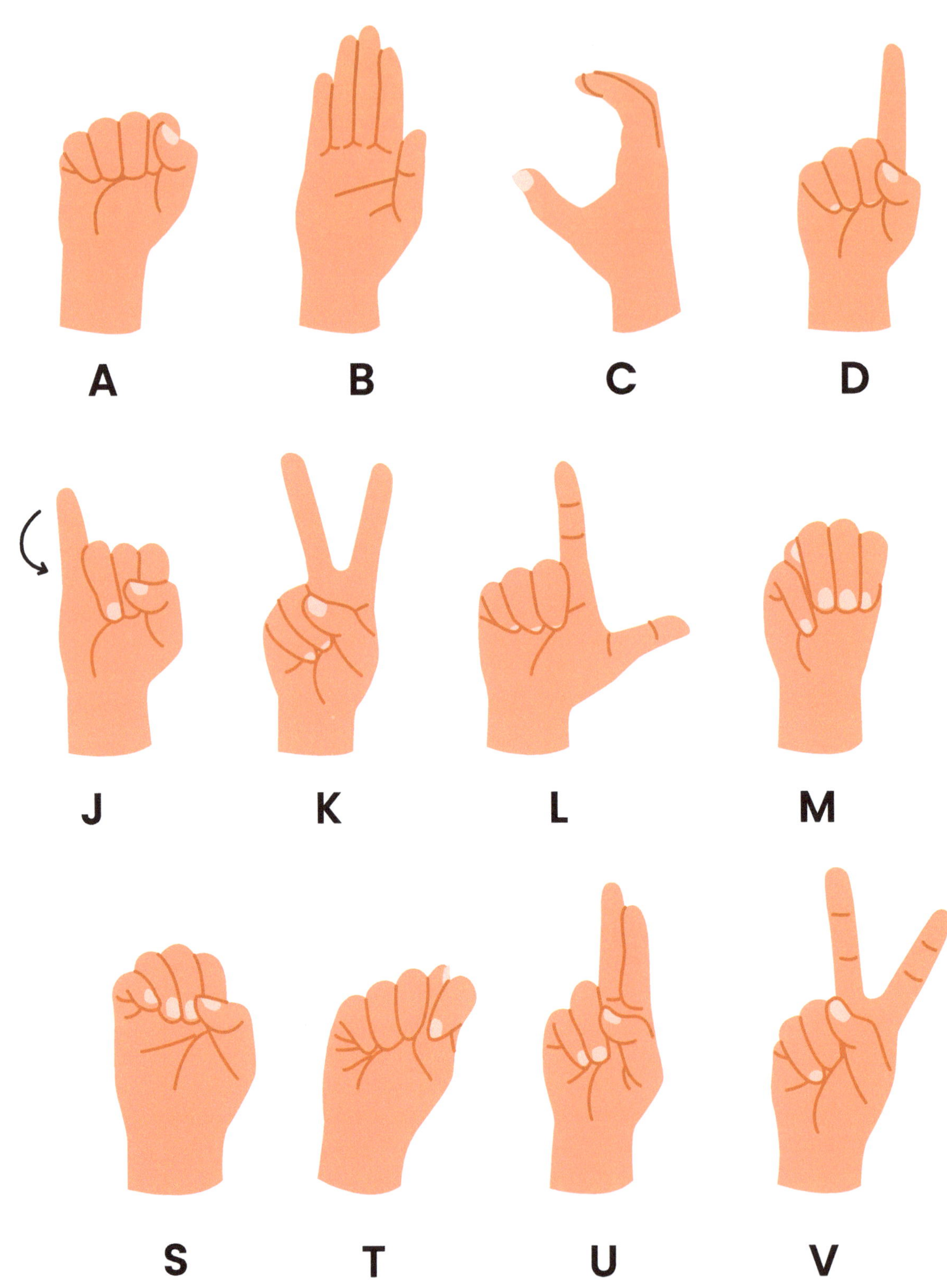

A
B
C
D
J
K
L
M
S
T
U
V

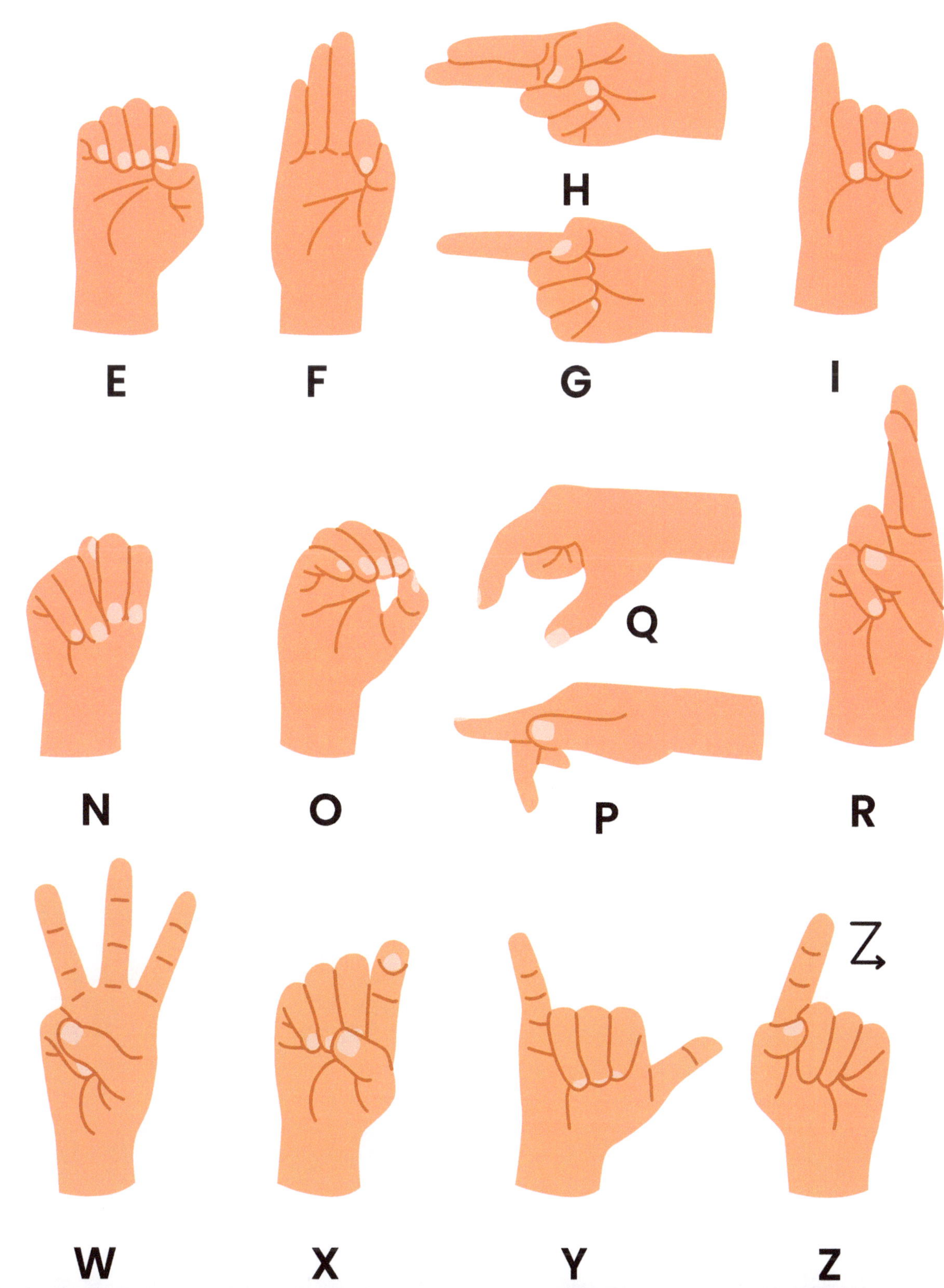

E
F
H
G
I
N
O
Q
P
R
W
X
Y
Z